Hampden

The Political State and Condition of her Majesty's Protestant

Subjects

In the Province of Quebec

Hampden

The Political State and Condition of her Majesty's Protestant Subjects
In the Province of Quebec

ISBN/EAN: 9783337183691

Printed in Europe, USA, Canada, Australia, Japan

Cover: Foto ©Suzi / pixelio.de

More available books at **www.hansebooks.com**

THE

Political State and Condition

OF

HER MAJESTY'S PROTESTANT SUBJECTS

IN

THE PROVINCE OF QUEBEC.

(SINCE CONFEDERATION.)

BY HAMPDEN

———•••———

"Some village Hampden, that with dauntless breast
The little tyrant of his fields withstood,
Some mute inglorious Milton here may rest ;
Some Cromwell, guiltless of his country's blood."

Grey's Elegy.

———•••———

TORONTO:

THE CANADIAN NEWS AND PUBLISHING CO.

1871.

THE POLITICAL STATE

OF

Her Majesty's Subjects in the Province of Quebec,

(SINCE CONFEDERATION.)

W HEN the Edict of Nantes, which had been granted to the Huguenots by Henry IV., of France in 1598, was revoked by Louis XIV. in 1685, the reformed or Calvinistic Protestants of that country abandoned their possessions, to seek in foreign lands that peace and contentment they looked for in vain in their own native homes. When they reached the mountains of the *Jura* in Switzerland, they threw themselves down on their knees and thanked God he had saved them from persecution and misery. Such will inevitably be the fate of the Protestants of the Province of Quebec, if they do not at once and forever stem the tide of intolerance and bigotry, which has been setting in for some time past and will eventually lead to the same sufferings and exile their ancestors endured in Calvinistic France. The French Canadians have no idea of the blessings of religious tolerance ; they cannot appreciate the world-wide benefits which accrue to all classes alike from a participation in equal rights, and social and religious liberty. Neither their moral nor intellectual education permits them to see the consequences of a blind bigotry, which must re-act against themselves, and from the effects of which they alone will be the sufferers, for they form a minority even on that narrow strip of land, which constitutes the northern portion of the Dominion on the banks of the St. Lawrence. It is hardly necessary to revert to the pages of Canadian history to prove, that ever since the conquest of Canada by the British arms, the battle of life, liberty, and happiness has been fought between the conquerors and the conquered. The English residents of Canada, who were once in a minority, treated their French Canadian fellow-countrymen with kindness, courtesy, and affability. From the administration of General Murray in 1760 down to that of Lord Gosford in 1835, they were the objects of the warmest solicitude and generosity, and the recipients of the most distinguished favors both on the part of the British Government and their fellow-colonists in Canada. In political government they shared the honors and responsibilities of office ; in their educational and industrial pursuits they were fostered and encouraged ; and in their social intercourse with their fellow-citizens they were on a footing of equality,—what more could they have desired ? The country at that period was sparsely populated ; the blessings of education were not so widespread as they are at present, and in comparison with the number of their educated and distinguished men, they shared equally with their English speaking fellow colonists in the honors and emoluments of office. It is true there were favorites of the home authorities in those days, who monopolized the largest share of colonial emoluments, but this was a grievance which was equally felt by the English and the French Canadian. If the experience of history teacheth the truth, it may be safely asserted (for the assertion is truthful), that in proportion to the number of offices which was conferred in the colony on *native born* colonists, the French Canadian surpassed his fellow-colonist of *native* English origin in the accumulation of the favors of Government. Did not Adam Lymburner and several of his fellow-colonists of British extraction at the period of the American Revolution, repair to the Island of Orleans and raise the standard of revolt, because they reproached the British Government with having conferred too many favors on their French Canadian fellow-countrymen? It would well repay the student of history to refer to the petition which was addressed to King George III., by the English colonists of that day, against the passing of the Imperial Statute of 1774, which guaranteed to the inhabitants of New France the exercise of their religion and the use of their language and laws. Canada was not then, nor has it ever since been, treated by the British Government as a conquered country. Look again at the pages of history and see how other nations have used their conquered or ceded territory, and to what purposes they have applied it ; they constituted it into penal colonies to which they condemned the vilest criminals and ruffians, with whom the conquered people would have to mix and associate —the swamps and torrid heat of Cayenne or French Guiana enured men from the prisons of France to the hardships of life, who were sent there to be a terror and a curse to the people ?

And how has England been repaid for the benefits she has conferred on her French Canadian subjects in the Province of Quebec? By their rising in open rebellion in 1837 and 1838 against her rightful power and authority ; by their massacre of Lieutenant Weir of Her Majesty's 32nd Regiment, and their attempted massacre of every man, woman, and child of British origin in the Province ; by their impotent threats of rebellion, if the union of the Provinces were not abolished and a local Parliament given to them ; and finally by the jesuitry they employed in making British statesmen believe, that by the confederation of the Provinces, the Protestant minority in the Province of Quebec would be guaranteed in the preservation of their rights, liberties, and properties. It is this last phase of their Machiavelian policy, which will be considered, and justly so, by posterity as the crowning act of their insincerity and hypocrisy in all their negotiations with the British Government. When they sought a federal and not a legislative union of the Provinces; when their representatives at the Westminster Hotel so beguiled the emissaries from this and other Provinces as to induce them to yield to their solicitations, they contemplated and projected the utter subserviency, not to say slavery, of over three hundred thousand Protestant and English Canadian colonists to nearly a million Roman Catholic and French Canadian inhabitants of the Province of Quebec. Under the cover of an assumed liberality, they caused to be introduced in the " British North America Act, 1867," the following section: —" The Legislative Assembly of Quebec shall be composed of " sixty-five members to be elected to represent the sixty-five

" electoral divisions or districts of Lower Canada in this Act
" referred to, subject to alteration thereof by the Legislature of
" Quebec, provided that it shall not be lawful to present to the
" Lieutenant-Governor of Quebec for assent any bill altering the
" limits of any of the electoral divisions or districts mentioned
"in the second schedule of this Act, unless the second and
" third readings of such Bill have been passed in the Legisla-
" tive Assembly with the concurrence of the majority of the
" members representing all those electoral divisions or districts,
" and the assent will not be given to such bill unless an address
" has been presented by the Legislative Assembly to the
" Lieutenant-Governor, stating that it has been so passed."

The electoral divisions or districts mentioned in the second
schedule to the Act of Confederation are the following :—
" Pontiac—Ottawa—Argenteuil—Huntingdon—Missisquoi—
" Brome—Shefford—Stanstead—Compton—Wolfe and Rich-
" mond—Megantic and the Town of Sherbrooke, twelve con-
"'stituencies in all." It may here be very appropriately asked,
why Montreal Centre, as well as Montreal West, was
excluded, and why the united Counties of Drummond and
Arthabaska were left out of the category ? The plain answer
is this, that many of the counties indicated in the second schedule were supposed, at the time confederation was being dis-
cussed, to be rapidly filling up with French Canadians, and that
under the influence and direction of the Roman Catholic
Clergy, there was an extensive emigration from the Canadian
parishes to those counties, and that the probability was, that in
a very few years, French Canadian representatives would out-

number those of English extraction, and so attain the object they had in view, viz., the disfranchisement of the English and Protestant community in the Province of Quebec. It required only seven French Canadians, to change the limits of those counties and incorporate them in other constituencies favorable to their political and religious views. Already under the ·beneficent working of the provisions of the Act, two out of the seven have been acquired by the dominant clergy—Jacques Picard, M.P.P. for Richmond and Wolfe, and Michel A. Bessette for Shefford, and how many others will follow the future will determine. To elucidate the mode in which they desire to speedily carry out the above recited provision of the Confederation Act, by which the Protestant element in the Legislative Assembly is to be virtually annihilated, it is barely necessary to allude to the result of the first election after Confederation for Richmond and Wolfe, at which Mr. Picard was elected by a scanty majority over his opponent, Mr. W. E. Jones, editor and proprietor of the Richmond Guardian. Justly fearing that Mr. Jones would be successful in the last election over his opponent Mr. Picard, the Government nominated the former a few months before the election as Emigration Agent to Europe, with instructions not to return until the month of August, which was after the election, so that in the interval his former opponent might be elected by acclamation !—and so he was ! and so will others be, until the number of seven delegates be returned to Parliament from the counties named in the second schedule of the· Confederation Act, and the disfranchisement of Protestants be successfully,carried out under the auspices of the Roman Catholic Clergy in the Legislative Assembly of the Province of Quebec.

And how has the Government of the Province of Quebec, selected its members of the Legislative Council of Quebec, under the provisions of the seventy-second section of the Act of Confederation ? It reads thus :—"The Legislative Council " of Quebec shall be composed of twenty-four members, to be " appointed by the Lieutenant-Governor in the Queen's name, "by instrument under the great seal of Quebec, one being "appointed to represent each of the twenty-four electoral di- " visions of Lower Canada in this Act referred to, and *each* *"holding office for the term of his life,* unless the Legislature of " Quebec otherwise provides under the provisions of this Act."

Of the twenty-four members of the Legislative Council, four only are Protestants, while in proportion to the probable population at the time of confederation, eight at least ought to have been chosen as the objects of the benevolence of Her Majesty through the intercession and recommendation of the Honorable Sir Narcisse Fortunat Belleau, Knight, Lieutenant-Governor of the Province of Quebec. Of fourteen officers of the Legislative Council, two alone are Protestants, and of thirty-six officers of the Legislative Assembly, there are but three who belong to that faith. It is immaterial whether the patronage rests with Mr. George Manly Muir, Clerk of the House, on whom Pope Pius IX. conferred the Order of St. Gregory, or on the dominant party in the Assembly, the fact remains the same, that of the officers, both of the Legislative Council and Legislative Assembly, one-third at least ought to profess the Protestant faith, as a measure of common honesty and justice towards, not the least respectable portion of Her Majesty's subjects in this part of her Dominion.

And what has been the distribution of the Queen's favors to other persons since confederation? While the noble, high-minded English speaking subject of Her Majesty is toiling with his usual perseverance and industry to add to his own means of living, and thereby increase the national capital and wealth of the country, the lazy, indolent, and impassive French Canadian jogs along in his usual way, hoping and trusting that by means of legislation, or the patronage of the Local Government, he may be enabled to obtain some lucrative office or employment, and thereby obtain a fancied position of superiority over his fellow-colonist of another origin. While since confederation the English speaking inhabitants of the Province of Quebec are entitled in fairness and justice to one-third of the honors and offices of Government, they are scarcely recognized in the distribution of Governmental patronage, and are, in fact, what the French Canadian father inculcates on the mind of his children, viz., strangers in their own country! As will be seen hereafter, this is not only a paternal, but a sacerdotal admonition which the priest as well as the parent impresses on the attention of his flock.

In educational and industrial pursuits the same rule is observed. If a law be passed respecting schools or agricultural societies, if any money is to be raised for the joint benefit of both Roman Catholic and Protestant, the superiority of the one, and the inferiority of the other, seems to be the guiding rule of action. Thus an amendment to the school laws was passed, conferring the power to tax corporate bodies for school purposes, according to the respective sects and denominations to which the shareholders may belong. Great care was taken to place the distribution of the monies in the hands of the Roman Catholic School Commissioners, to whom the Protestants were to apply for their *pro rata* of the contribution coming to them. Again, if the Dissentient wishes to pay his school taxes for the support of Dissentient Schools, he is obliged to notify the Roman Catholic School Commissioners that such is his intention, and so the cases, wherein the rule of superiority prevails, might be multiplied *ad infinitum*, showing the spirit of French Canadian legislation in a country, which in name alone is a British colony.

And if the place of a high officer of Government should become vacant, who is chosen to fill it ? Not the moral, religious Protestant, who fears God and honors the Queen, and who believes his whole duty to consist in conscientiously performing his duty to his fellow-men, but the renegade and the convert, or one whose brother is in Holy Orders in the Roman Catholic Church. It is sufficient as a mere semblance of justice that he be a Protestant in name, although he be really a Roman Catholic in heart. Late appointments to some of the highest offices in the Province of Quebec afford striking proof of the truth of this remark.

The preamble to the British North America Act, 1867, *federally* uniting the Provinces into one Dominion, reading thus, " Whereas such a union would conduce to the welfare of " the Provinces and promote the interests of the British Em- " pire," it ought very naturally to have been expected that at the outset of Confederation a spirit of moderation and of justice would prevail in the Councils of each separate Province ; that the rights, interests, and even the jealousies of minorities would be respected and regarded ; that if sectarian legislation were required, it would be enacted to such a moderate extent, that no one could complain ; and that full and ample justice should be done, irrespective of nationality, origin, or creed.

There is a manliness in the character of the Briton, which would teach him to repudiate any undue assumption of author- ity over any class, and thus we had until lately failed to observe any complaints on the part of the Roman Catholic minority in Ontario against the action of the governing power. The Pro- testant Episcopacy and Clergy of that Province have too much self-respect and too much regard for toleration and equal rights even to think for a moment of interfering with the political and religious rights of their Roman Catholic brethren. Born and brought up in close affinity and relationship with persons of all classes and denominations, they would scorn to take advantage which their numbers might justify them to do, over the weak and the powerless. They are men who appreciate too highly the blessings of civil and religious liberty, ever to deny to others that which they prize so much themselves.

How is it with us in Her Majesty's Province of Quebec ? how has it been for years past, and particularly since Confeder- ation ? The burden was hard enough to bear under the Union

Act of 1841. Such was the vacillation and time serving policy of every successive ministry ; such was the desire of both the ministerialist and the oppositionist to gain the political aid of the French Canadian party, as it was called, that the social and general interests of the English minority in Lower Canada were neglected, if not contemned. The Israelites of Egypt never had harder taskmasters in the persons of the Pharoahs, than had the English Canadians at the hands of the Clergy, at whose beck and nod the French Canadian portion of the Ministry of the day would pass any law, heedless of its consequences to British interests or British feeling. But they never went so far as they have done *since* Confederation ; the wounds they then inflicted could be cauterized ; they entered the body, not the soul,—they never advocated a state of moral degradation comparatively with which the condition of the slave of the South was to be envied. They did not suggest the total prohibition of the Protestant to exercise the rights of suffrage ; they did not exclude him from taking part in the work of legislation ; they did not consider him like the Pariah of old, as a sore and a leper in society ; finally, they did not arrogate to themselves the right of interfering in the domestic ,affairs of the family circle, controlling, if not destroying, the happiness of the home.

It is not inopportune here to remark, that nearly one half of the business in our Legislative Assembly consists, in the passing of laws affecting Roman Catholic interests or incorporating religious and eleemosynary institutions. In every city, town, village, or hamlet, in the Province of Quebec, the most valuable property is placed in mortmain by Act of Parliament, and held untaxed ; not content with this they repeat the history of Naboth and his vineyard. Lest the reader of this pamphlet may not be well versed in Scriptural lore, its transcription in language easy to be comprehended may not be misplaced. It is taken from the 1st Kings xxi.

Closely adjoining Ahab's palace in Israel was a beautiful vineyard, belonging to a man of the name of Naboth. This property was coveted by the King, who sent for Naboth and said to him, " Give me thy vineyard, that I may have it for a garden of herbs, because it is near my house, and I will give thee for it a better vineyard; or, if it seems good to thee, I will give thee the worth of it in money." But Naboth would not surrender the ground ; it was dear to him because he had inherited it from his father, and he refused all offers however tempting. Then Ahab went into his house dejected and displeased. He, the great monarch, had been baulked of his desire by one of his subjects ; so " he lay upon his bed and turned away his face and would not eat." Not long afterwards came Jezebel, fierce and malignant as ever. She pressed Ahab to tell her what troubled him. and when she heard his complaint, she exclaimed indignantly, " Dost thou not govern the Kingdom of Israel ? Arise and eat bread and let thy heart be merry. I will give thee the vineyard of Naboth the Jezreelite.

Then Jezebel wrote letters in Ahab's name and sealed them with his seal, and sent them herself to the elders and nobles of the city. She commanded their chiefs to proclaim a fast, to set Naboth high among the people, and to bring forward two men to testify that he had uttered blasphemies against God and the King ; and then upon their accusations to stone him to death. The elders obediently executed the commands of the ruthless queen. Two wicked men were easily found to bear false witness against Naboth. He was declared guilty, and stoned to death before the gates of the city. When this foul deed was accomplished, Jezebel went triumphantly to her husband and bade him arise and take possession of the vineyard which he had desired, and which Naboth would not sell him for money. The weak monarch arose from his couch and went forth into his ill-gotten vineyard. There he was confronted by that well known form shrouded in a rough hairy mantle, and he heard again the voice of Elijah the Tishbite : " Hast thou killed also and taken possession ? Thus says the Lord, in the place where dogs licked the blood of Naboth shall dogs lick thy blood, even thine." Then Ahab exclaimed in fear, "Hast thou found me, O my enemy ?" The answer of Elijah conveyed to the terrified monarch the awful doom which awaited his entire house : " The dogs shall eat Jezebel by the wall of Jezreel; him that dies of Ahab in the city the dogs shall eat ; and him that dies in the field the fowls of the air shall eat." Ahab, alarmed by these words, was struck with remorse and contrition ; he rent his clothes and put sackcloth on his body. " And the word of the Lord came to Elijah the Tishbite, saying, seest thou how Ahab humbles himself before Me? because he humbles himself before Me, I will not bring the evil in his days ; but in his son's days will I bring the evil upon his house."

2

In considering the actual state and condition of the Protestants in the Province of Quebec, arising out of the anomalous position which was imposed upon them for State purposes in the confederation of the North American Colonies, it will hardly be necessary to revert to those general principles and ordinary maxims, which are firmly fixed in the mind of every enlightened person. Charity and benevolence towards all, or in other words, " Peace on earth and good will to all men," are the maxims which, in every country and in every age, have distinguished the tolerant and the just. Locke, in his admirable Essays concerning the human understanding, puts this sentiment in such strong language, that its repetition will be excused. In speaking of mutual charity and forbearance, he says (volume 2nd, page 279, chapter 16, section 4, on Degrees of Assent)— " It is unavoidable to the greatest part of men, if not all, to have several opinions, without certain and indubitable proofs of their truths ; and it carries too great an imputation of ignorance, lightness and folly, for men to quit and renounce their former tenets presently upon the offer of an argument which they cannot immediately answer and show the insufficiency of. It would, we think, become all men to maintain *peace and the common offices of humanity and friendship in the diversity of opinions,* since we cannot reasonably expect that any one should readily and obsequiously quit his own opinion and embrace ours, with a blind resignation to an authority, which the understanding of men acknowledges not. For, however, it may often mistake, it can own no other guide but reason, nor blindly submit to the will and dictates of another." And

he asks, with an air of triumph worthy of the great philoso-
pher and profound thinker, "Where is the man that has incontestable evidence of the truth of all that he holds, or of the
falsehood of all he condemns ; or can say that he has examined
to the bottom all his own or other men's opinions ?"

The reader will very naturally inquire for the proofs of the
denunciations against the Roman Catholic Clergy, and of their
hostility to the cause of Protestantism in Quebec. Every man
is a witness of the acts which fall under his own observation,
and no one will gainsay anything that has been advanced, who
has in his own person suffered the untimely interference of the
priesthood in matters of concern to himself alone. Nor are
there many who have the courage and determination to dare
confront those who, in the height of their power and influence,
have interfered in their domestic affairs or thwarted their efforts
to gain a livelihood for themselves or their families. But for-
tunately the proofs are at hand, and it will not require much
research to establish the fact that, in the late elections for members to represent the constituencies in the Legislative Assembly,
they have shown the cloven foot and evinced their deep-seated
hostility to every one who is a Protestant in the Province of
Quebec. The following is a correct translation of the *Roman
Catholic Programme*, which was extensively circulated throughout the Province of Quebec during the late elections :—

CATHOLIC PROGRAMME.

THE APPROACHING ELECTIONS..

" Our country, submitted to a constitutional rule, will, in a short time, have to choose its representatives. This simple fact necessarily raises a question, which our duty obliges us to settle, and this question should be put as follows :

What should be the course pursued by Catholic electors in the controversy, which is about taking place, and what should be their line of conduct in the choice of candidates, who will solicit their suffrages ?

We believe we can answer this question in a satisfactory manner by affording some development to the ideas expressed by his Grace, the Lord Bishop of Three Rivers in his last Pastoral letter.

Here are the words which we find therein :—

" *The men whom you send to represent you in the Legislature are required to protect and defend your religious interests, according to the spirit of the Church, as well as to promote and protect your temporal interests, for civil laws are necessarily in relation on a great number of points with religion.   It is what the fathers of the council plainly said in their decree.*

You should therefore prudently assure yourselves that the candidate to whom you give your suffrage is duly qualified on both these points, and that he offers, morally speaking, all suitable guarantees for the protection of these grave interests.

We ought, without doubt, to render thanks to God for the full and entire liberty the constitution grants, by right, to the Catholic faith to regulate and govern itself conformably to the rules of the Church. It is by a judicious choice of your Legislators that you will assure to yourselves the preservation and enjoyment of that liberty: the most precious of all, and which should give to your chief Pastors the immense advantage of being able to govern the Church of Canada under the immediate advice and directions of the Holy See and of the Romish Church, the mother and the mistress of all the churches.

These counsels dictated by wisdom will, we trust, be understood by all the Catholic electors of the Province of Quebec. It is impossible to deny that politics are closely bound up with religion, *and that the separation of the Church and the State is an absurd and impious doctrine.* This is particularly true of the constitutional rule, which attributing to Parliament all power of legislation, places in the hands of those who compose it a double-edged weapon which might become terrible.

It is for this it becomes necessary : that those who exercise this Legislative authority should be in perfect harmony with the teachings of the Church. It is for this it is the duty of Catholic electors to choose for their representatives men whose principles are perfectly sound and sure.

The full and entire adhesion to Roman Catholic doctrines, in religious politics and social economy should be the first and principal qualification that Catholic electors should exact from the Catholic candidate. It is the safest criterion of which they can avail themselves to judge of men and things. We understand there can be no question here of Protestants to whom we leave the same liberty which we claim for ourselves !

These premises being established, it is easy to deduce the consequences, which will serve as a guide to the electors. But in order to establish practical rules, the application of which will be easy, we must take into account the particular circumstances, in which our country is placed, the political parties which are formed therein and their antecedents.

We belong in principle to the conservative party ; that is to say, to that which constituted itself the defender of social authority. It is sufficient to say, that by the conservative party, we do not mean every set of men who have no other tie than that of personal interest and ambition; but a group of men sincerely professing the same principles of religion and nationality, preserving in their integrity the traditions of the old conservative party, which may be summed up in an inviolable attachment to Catholic doctrines, and an absolute devotion to the national interests of Lower Canada.

In the political situation of our country, the conservative party being the only one which offers serious guarantees to religious interests, we regard it as a duty to honestly support the men placed at its head.

But this loyal support *must be subordinate to religious interests which we ought never to lose sight of.* If, therefore, there exist in our laws any defect, ambiguities, or provisions which place in peril the interests of Catholics, we should exact a formal engagement from our candidates to work, in order to cause these defects in our Legislation to disappear.

For instance, the religious press complains, with reason, that our laws on marriage, education, the erection of parishes, and registers of the civil *status*, are defective, inasmuch as they injure the rights of the Church, restrain its liberty, trammel its administration, or may lead to hostile interpretations. This state of things imposes on Catholic members the duty of changing and modifying them, as . our Holinesses the Bishops of the Province may demand, in order to put them in harmony with the doctrines of the Roman Catholic Church. Therefore, that members may acquit themselves more diligently of this duty, the electors should make it a condition of their support. It is the duty of the electors not to give their suffrages but to those who will entirely conform to the instructions of the Church in these matters.

Let us, therefore, conclude to adopt certain general rules in certain given cases.

1. If the contestation should take place between two conservatives, there can be no question that we should support the one who will accept the programme which we have just traced out.

2. If, on the contrary, it should take place between a conservative of any color, and an adept of the *liberal school*, our active sympathies should be for the former.

3. If the only candidates who offer themselves for our suffrages in a constituency are all liberals or oppositionists, we should choose him *who will subscribe to our conditions.*

4. Finally, in a case where the contestation occurs between a conservative rejecting our programme and an oppositionist, even should he accept it, the case will be more delicate.

To vote for the first will be to place us in opposition with the doctrine which we have just now exposed. To vote for the second would be to place the conservative party in danger, which we desire to see powerful. What part should we take between these two dangers? We should then advise the withdrawal of Catholic electors.

It must be, nevertheless, understood that these rules which are laid down leave to the electors a certain liberty of action, which will depend on the particular circumstances of each constituency, and the antecedents of each candidate. *Besides, we have only tried to show the religious convictions and qualifications which the electors ought to exact from those who solicit their suffrages.* It is right to add, that to make their religious convictions prevail, it is necessary the members should be learned and intelligent. After being certain of the religious principles of the candidates, it is in the second place necessary there should be the largest possible amount of learning and intelligence in the House.

We should, therefore, disapprove of every Ministerial Act which would tend to exclude from the Parliamentary arena, men who are capable of rendering service to the Catholic and National cause, under the pretext that they would restrain certain ambitions !

To constitute the representation of manageable and powerless ciphers would be certainly a great evil, which it would be necessary to avoid.

In two words, we wish to protect at the same time the honor of the country and the liberty of the Church, and all our programme may be summed up in this motto, "Religion and Country."

On the 6th June last, the Bishop of Montreal formally approved of the programme in the following words:—"The present is to certify to him who wishes to hear it, that I approve of the *Catholic Programme* on every point, and that there is nothing in this programme, which, in my opinion, is worthy of blame, even on the score of its timeliness. I add that I consider this programme as the strongest protection of the true Conservative party and the firmest support of the good principles which should govern a Christian society. I attach myself to this principle, for I see in it the safety of my dear country, which will not be truly free unless the liberty of the Church shall be respected with all the rights which shall be assured and guaranteed to it.

(Signed), "JG. EV DE MONTREAL."

The Bishop of Three Rivers approved of it on the following day in these words :—" You ask me if my last circular letter contains an approbation of the Catholic Programme. As I spoke to be understood, I believe that no one can be mistaken, and that you see therein my approbation. I approved of it because I found the object of it to be good and legitimate, and that the means proposed to attain that object are just and honest.

(Signed),   " L. F. Ev. DE TROIS RIVIERES."

It was on the 20th April last that the Programme was first published, and it was afterwards very widely circulated in hand-bills throughout the Province. On the 21st it was published in the *Ordre* and the *Nouveau Monde*, and on the 23rd in the *Courier du Canada*, all of them organs of the Catholic Church. On the 24th April the Archbishop of Quebec issued a circular letter to his Clergy, in which, without disapproving of it, he said, " I believe it my duty to inform you that this programme only became known to me through the medium of the press, and that consequently it has the grievous inconvenience of having been drawn up without the participation of the Episcopacy." The Bishops of St. Hyacinthe and Rimouski also *faintly* disapproved of it. Hence arose a dispute between certain journals, whether the Laity could arrogate to themselves powers which could only be exercised by the Episcopacy. In fact, the Archbishop and his co-adjutors the Bishops of St. Hyacinthe and Rimouski saw the bad consequences of its publication in the journals at that particular time, and *apparently* blamed the two recalcitant Bishops, viz., of Montreal and Three Rivers, for countenancing it.

It is, however, very clear that the doctrines contained therein had been previously promulgated among the faithful, although they had not obtained such a wide circulation as that which is afforded through the columns of public journals. The organs of the Church did not venture to say that any of the Bishops disapproved of it, but merely confined themselves to the assertion, that its publication, coming from the Laity, was unauthorized. In fact, the same doctrines had been promulgated as far back as 1866, while Confederation was being mooted, and probably earlier—a fact which was cognizant to all the Bishops and Clergy in the Province, although the Bishop of Montreal may have no doubt regarding its timeliness, and the Archbishop of Quebec and his colleagues of St. Hyacinthe and Rimouski, may regret its unwise and untimely publication.

Here it may be advisable to make a short digression, and inquire into the state and condition of the English speaking portion of the population of the Province of Quebec, most of whom are Protestants, although they vary in their nationality, origin, and creed. Thus, there are English, Irish, and Scotch Protestants. The empires and kingdoms of Europe yield their contingent, and the French Canadian also (although few in number), combine to make up a solid and compact body, scattered in every part of the Province, but all animated by a common spirit, and working for a common cause : they are remarkable for their high intelligence, unswerving integrity, unceasing perseverance, and indomitable courage. The French

Canadian and Roman Catholic boasts of over two hundred and fifty years *national existence* in Lower Canada ; the British Protestant of not much more than half that period, during which he has abided here as a colonist, amidst all the toils and troubles, injuries, and persecutions incidental to living among French Canadians, who are numerically stronger ; and yet, speaking in general terms, what is their position comparatively, as regards commercial wealth and industrial enterprise? To say the least, two-thirds of the capital of Canada are furnished by the Protestant community, and are embarked in national enterprises, both on sea and land, the benefits of which are equally shared by the Catholic and Protestant. While the French Canadian is building churches and monasteries, the English Canadian is constructing ships and warehouses, not that he neglects the former, although he gives his attention to the latter. The munificent donations which have been made by Protestants for charitable and educational objects, vie with, if they do not greatly surpass, the amount of hard earned money of the poor, which has been wrested from them in the shape of tithes for purposes of a similar nature.

" *Nil sine magna vita labore dedit mortalibus.*"
—Horace Satires, Book 1st, 9th

In a political and social point of view, how different their condition, how debased !—how vile !—The French Canadian looks upon them as intruders on their national inheritance ; they would, if they could, spurn them from the soil, and if in the display of an honorable ambition, they seek for nomination to office under the Crown, their claim is looked upon as presumptuous and unreasonable. There have been instances (few and far between), since Confederation, where Protestants have been named to minor offices under the Government; but for one who has received a mark of favor, how many others of the other nationality and religion have been the recipients of the honors and favors of Government?

To resume the discussion of the political and religious principles, which were at work in the preparation of the *Programme* of the Catholic Church.

To do this satisfactorily, it is necessary to thoroughly comprehend the peculiar opinions of the Clergy and Laity of the Romish Church in Canada, on matters of nationality, religion, politics, and social economy. This is only to be derived from the study of the incipient literature of the country, and the opinions expressed by the well-educated class, who reside in the cities. There is a vagueness and want of uniformity in their ideas, which paralyze any deep inquiry into the subject. They have no well defined notions either on civil government or social economy. Their whole creed consists in the supposed connection between Church and State, without having any fixed idea of the line of demarcation which should exist between them. The works of Garneau, Ferland, Faillon, Bibaud, and others inculcate the belief that they have a divine mission to accomplish, that of founding and establishing a nation on the banks of the St. Lawrence, a belief which is re-echoed in the pulpit, in their literary associations, and at their public meetings. They never fail to impress on the minds of their hearers that they are a nation within a nation; that is to say, they were sent as the emissaries of Providence to establish their religion, laws, and institutions in this country, under the protection of the French Government, with the ultimate view of founding a nation in America. They say, " We have, as a nation, a mission to fulfil, and, as a people, an end to attain ; for there is no blank in the works of God. Each individual in the family, each family in the nation, each nation among men, have a post assigned to them beforehand. Let each one reach it by the ways which Providence has laid open to him, and this under the penalty of the most terrible punishments in case of prevarication, under pain of extermination and death for the individual, the family or the nation, who will obstinately refuse to march towards the end which he should attain, and accomplish his mission?" What is, therefore, the mission of the Canadian people ? They answer, the mission imposed on our fathers was the conversion and civilization of the savages of this country ; and the end which Divine Providence assigned to them was nothing less than the establishment of a people *profoundly Catholic in this land, which was given to them as an inheritance.*"

To reach this conclusion, they indulge in the wildest vagaries, in the most pellucid hallucinations. No chimera of the human mind was ever so absurd as the idea they entertain on this subject. There is a similarity between the fanaticism of the Mormon and the French Canadian on this point, which would strike the most careless observer. One of their most able writers, a Bishop in the Church, has lately published a work, wherein, without speaking metaphorically, he pertinaciously insists that Jacques Cartier was sent by the Almighty, as Abraham was sent from Mesopotamia, to point out to them the promised land, which was the Valley of the St. Lawrence! He profanely asserts that almost every incident in the lives of the Patriarchs, from the departure of Abraham from his country to the exodus from Egypt, and the arrival in the promised land, has been repeated, under Divine sanction, in the life of Jacques Cartier, Champlain, and others. What a vile profanation! what an unhallowed use of God's Holy Word! The antithesis in the narrative seems to be that, Abraham, full of faith and obedience, prepared to leave his country—whither, he knew not—it was enough for him that he left a land of superstition and idolatry to seek a new country, wherein he could worship the true God; while Jacques Cartier left a land of learning and piety, and a people of fame and culture (for Calvinism prevailed in France at that day), to found a colony on the banks of the St. Lawrence, where superstition and ignorance prevail to an extent unequalled in any other part of the world.

The only *hiatus* in the learned Bishop's argument in favor of the Divine mission seems to consist of this : that when Jacques Cartier was unable to procure recruits to follow him in his expedition to Canada, he applied to Francis I., who told him he might take the prisoners who were condemned to death in the prisons of France, but he would not permit any more of his subjects to leave the country. There are some historians who are malevolent enough to insinuate that Jacques Cartier acceded to the King's proposition, and brought out with him several of these malefactors, who remained in Canada, and permanently settled here. Another interposition of Divine Providence *in favor* of the Holy Mission of Jacques Cartier was the not less singular idea which entered the head of Henry IV., or rather of Henry of Navarre, as he was called, to entrust the care and execution of the plan of founding a colony in Canada to Chauvin the Calvinist, which, as he says, *providentially failed !*

The love of country is the noblest feeling in the human breast. The wildest Arab who wanders over the deserts of Arabia, or the savage in our western forests, would not, for all the world, leave his tent in the wilderness to enter the boundaries of civilization, nor would. he exchange the habits to which he has been enured from youth for those of civilized life. Denizens of the plain and the forest, they have an abiding sense of the charms of their own native wilds—the one takes as much delight in the chase of the lion and the tiger, as the other does in that of the moose and the bear—the arid sands of the desert, and the lakes and rivers of the forest, are the attractions to which Nature has allured them.

Man, also, in a state of civilization, has a natural desire to abide in or return to the home of his birth ; the love of country is implanted in his breast, as it is in all others, and leads him to perform the most brilliant actions in war, and the greatest achievements in science and arts in peace. This is the strongest bond of nationality—it is the tie which keeps nations together. But what nation, Asiatic, European, or American, would desire to confine the blessings they enjoy to themselves alone ? to practice that egotism and selfishness which would incline them to exclude others from the benefits they enjoy. The French Canadian is alone in his desire for isolation and retirement. He says if you are not with us you are against us, you must assist us in carrying out the ends of the Divine Mission—that is to say, to establish our religion, our laws, and institutions in this our promised land, or otherwise we shall blot you out and persecute you, as our forefathers in France did your ancestors of old.

And what of the Flag of England, with its bright and glorious aureole surrounding and emblazoning it? Did it twice wave for nothing on the hills of Cape Diamond in 1628, and 1759? Was the blood which was spilt in those memorable years, and which soddened the graves of as brave a set of men as ever carried arms, shed for nothing? Or was it spent to found a nation in Canada, who never cease vituperating and cursing the name of England? In their writings, in their daily intercourse, the French Canadian never ceases to hurl defiance at the conqueror who prevented them from accomplishing the Divine Mission—at that period—which they seek to do at the present day. Hear them speak of England's conduct towards Ireland. One of their eminent men and celebrated writers says, " Even the most powerful empires have rarely succeeded in completely denationalizing the unfortunate people with whom they are incorporated. Nevertheless, their annals have enregistered the most crying injustice and atrocious persecution, vainly exercised, to attain that object. These efforts nearly always frustrated themselves against the force of resistance, while unity of faith and of language conferred on these unfortunate populations. It is even a sight which has been given us to contemplate in the days in which Providence has placed our existence. Contemporary history daily narrates the revolting conduct of England to anglify and protestantize faithful Ireland, and the sanguinary barbarism of Russia to denationalize and decatholocize heroic Poland." * * * In speaking of the immorality and frightful consequences of a policy founded on any other basis than justice and equity, he continues his diatribes against England and Protestantism in the following words :—" But should heroic Poland or faithful Ireland ever so much desire to alleviate the weight of the yoke which burdens them, without, however, the aid of revolution and denouncing all solidarity *with those cosmopolites without faith nor law*, they would treat the most courageous of their children as rebels, or send them to expiate the crime of having wished to restore liberty to their dear country, on the gallows; or confine them in dark dungeons ; or subject them to the torments of an exile worse even than death itself."

And this is the language of a spiritual pastor of the Roman Catholic Church, the warm supporter and friend of the Minister of Militia and his followers in the House of Commons of this Dominion; and of a pastor who has unbounded influence on the minds of thousands and tens of thousands of his French Canadian fellow countrymen !

As these lines are being written (the 12th July—an ominous day !) news is conveyed over the telegraph wires that in the electoral contest for the representation of the united Counties of Drummond and Arthabaska in the Legislative Assembly,

Edward I. Hemming, Esq., the late representative, has been defeated by Wilfred Laurier, Esq., by the overwhelming majority of nearly a thousand votes. What brought this about? Mr. Hemming was a devoted adherent of the Provincial Ministry, supported them in all their measures, and did as much as he could *consistently* do, to further the views of the dominant party. Whence, therefore, the cause? It is the most striking proof that can be afforded of the efficacy of the Programme as far as nationality is concerned. Mr. Hemming is a Protestant . and his adversary a Catholic.

Having disposed of the question of nationality ; that is to say, having shown that if the French Canadians are not in the eyes of the world a separate and distinct nation, they consider themselves so, it will be necessary to look at the expression of the political views of the authors of the *Programme*.

It is an incontestable fact, that the foundation stone of their national edifice reposes on a belief in Church and State. To borrow again from the works of the distinguished prelate, to whom allusion has already been made, he says : " To *watch and control* legislative action in the enactment of all necessary laws for the good government of the people ; to *watch and control* (the italics are his own) all the acts of Governmental administration ; here are certainly very great privileges and very serious rights ; but for those who enjoy these privileges and exercise these rights the responsibility is very heavy, I might almost say fearful for him who understands all their weight and extent."

To watch and *control* all the acts of Governmental administration would imply that this could not be legitimately done by the legislator ; if so, it must be done very indirectly by means of his votes in Parliament. The impression would be conveyed and certain facts bear out its truth, that it is the Church, either directly or through the Legislator, that *controls* the administrative acts of Government.

During the Quebec Conference, before Confederation, the question of divorce was raised. It was very naturally a subject of inquiry, whether the concession of this right to the Federal Parliament would not militate against the rights of the Church. The Catholic members at the Conference, knowing the power which Confederation would confer on the Church in the Province of Quebec, and foreseeing the humiliation, not to say destruction, of the Protestant element in the population of the Province, *seemed* readily to consent to the proposition ; nevertheless, they had certain doubts on the point, and the present Archbishop of Quebec, who was then Rector of the Laval University, either proceeded to Rome or communicated with the Papal authorities on the subject. He asked them if a Catholic could conscientiously, under the circumstances in which the French Canadians then found themselves in Canada, or a Catholic member of Parliament, sustain by his vote the project of Confederation, such as it had emanated from the Quebec Conference ?

All the high officers of the Church were consulted ; the College of Cardinals, the members of the Propaganda, the Pope himself for aught that is known, and the answer, strange to say, was in the affirmative. They were willing to sacrifice all their preconceived ideas on the sanctity of the marriage tie, of its being a sacrament which nothing could destroy, in order to obtain political pre-eminence over the English Canadian and the Protestant in the Province of Quebec. The prize was too great to be jeopardized and possibly lost by a blind adherence to a doctrine, which for ages had been a fundamental one in the Church of Rome. Secrets, communicated confidentially, alone interpose a barrier against revealing other acts of the members, both of the Federal and Local Governments of Quebec, wherein they were counselled by the clergy as to the line of action they should follow in the administrative departments of their respective Governments.

The *Programme* says : " It is impossible to deny that politics are closely bound up with religion, and that the separation of the Church and the State is an absurd and impious doctrine. This is particularly true of our Constitutional Government, which, attributing to Parliament all power of legislation, places in the hands of those who compose it a double-edged weapon, which might become terrible."

What do the authors of the *Programme* mean ? Do they insinuate that, not content with depriving the Protestant of the right to interfere in the business of legislation, they would introduce into the Province of Quebec the institution of Loyola, or the *Monita Secreta* of Laynez or Aquaviva ? What is that double-edged weapon which is to become so terrible ? Will it affect the soul or the body ? Is the thumb-screw to be applied mentally or physically ?

When a considerable class in enlightened England doubt the

propriety and expediency of a connection between Church and
State, when they would desire to see the spiritual heads of the
Church removed from their seats in the House of Lords, it is
rather strange that in free America any body of men should be
found, who would assert that the separation of the Church and
State was an absurd and impious doctrine. It is true, that
since the union of the Provinces in 1841, the period when responsible Government was introduced, it has been well known
that the Church in the Province of Quebec has exercised an
unwise influence in matters of a temporal nature, yet it is only
lately they have become so outspoken on the subject ; they now
openly declare that religion being intimately connected with
politics, it behoves them to assert the doctrine as being an in-
tegral part of their religious and political faith. They go far-
ther, and in both their writings and conversation insinuate that
none but Catholics should participate in the business of government or legislation in the Province. It is true that in a very
few instances Protestants have succeeded in being elected in
Roman Catholic constituencies, but under such terms and conditions that they forfeit their own self-respect and the respect
and consideration of their co-religionists. In some cases they
have been compelled to make concessions on matters of faith,
humiliating to their consciences and detrimental to the position
in which they would desire to be held by their English-speaking
fellow-countrymen. No consideration of superior ability to
discharge legislative functions, no idea of liberality or justice
towards him whom they admit to be better qualified than themselves to perform them, would induce the French Canadian to

swerve from the objects he has in view, that of founding a great Catholic nation in the Valley of the St. Lawrence. One of their writers says : " We conclude from the legislative action of Protestants in matters of divorce, common schools, usury and intemperance, that it is the duty of every Catholic elector to be assured that the man whom he votes for will always act in his capacity as the representative of a Catholic constituency, and *will vote conformably to the principles of the Catholic Church.* Any candidate who will not accept such a condition ought to frankly declare it to his electors, if he be honest, and not accept an office which would not have been conferred upon him, excepting on that condition. * * * He adds, for the French Canadian elector, whom we know to be a Catholic above all, the candidate of his choice should be one, who would offer the greatest guarantee for the protection and defence of his faith, his language and national institutions." He cites the seventeenth chapter of Deuteronomy, 14th and 15th verses : "When thou art come unto the land, which the Lord thy God giveth thee, and shalt possess it, and shalt dwell therein, and shalt say, ' I will set a King over me, like as all the nations that are about me.' Thou shalt in any wise set him King over thee, whom the Lord thy God shall choose ; *one from among thy brethren shalt thou set King over thee; thou mayest not set a stranger over thee, who is not thy brother.*"

In matters of social economy, the Programme would imply that the rights, immunities and privileges of the Roman Church are not sufficiently protected by existing laws. It says, " That the religious press complains with reason, that our laws on marriage education, the erection of parishes, and registers of civil *status*, are defective, inasmuch as they injure the rights of the Church, restrain its liberty, trammel its administration, and may lead to hostile interpretations."

As regards marriage, it has been a matter of complaint that several articles were inserted in the Civil Code of Lower Canada, authorizing the nullity of the marriage tie in certain specified cases and that they militate against the right of the ecclesiastical authorities to exercise exclusive jurisdiction over such matters according to the canons of their Church. Should the law be altered the greatest evils might follow. For instance, many marriages are contracted in the Province of Quebec between Protestants and Roman Catholics, which are solemnized by a minister of the former or a priest of the latter faith. The Civil Code regards marriage more in the light of a civil contract than a religious one. In the eyes of the Church, it is a sacrament which no rule can effect nor no law abrogate. Yet it is contended by some persons, and they are not a few, that such marriages, when celebrated by a Protestant minister, are illegal and are not binding on the Catholic husband or wife, as the case may be. Now, if the Church had the power, which it arrogates to itself, to declare such marriages illegal by virtue of their ecclesiastical laws, the children of such marriages (if the laws were altered) would be illegitimate, and consequently deprived of their right of inheritance. There are other cases enumerated in the Civil Code, wherein the marriage tie might be dissolved by the tribunals, which would impair the rights of the Church. It is for this they seek the abrogation of these laws, it behoves the Protestant community, within the Province of Quebec, to watch with jealousy any innovation which might tend to impair the security they now enjoy, or to affect the interests of families which to them may be so much at heart. With unwearied vigilance and unceasing appeals to the common sense of the more liberal among the French Canadian representatives they may avert evils, the consequences of which would be experienced not alone by themselves but by their children after them.

With respect to the national reforms they seek to enact, surely the present laws on the subject afford them every protection and safeguard they require. The numerical majority the French Canadians possess in the Legislature of the Province enables them to make any alterations they may desire in the existing regulations, provided these do not affect the rights of the Dissentients, for if they did, the 93rd section of the British North American Act fully protects the latter against any innovations. What, then, do they require to make these defects in their educational institutions the subject of remonstrances in their religious journals? Do they wish to pass laws in defiance of guaranteed rights and well-established privileges, or do they think that the appeal mentioned in that section of the Act must be exercised by the Parliament, over which they have exclusive and paramount control? They hold that the parent must yield to the clergy in the supervision of the education of his child; that family interests must yield to secular ones; and that the Church alone possesses the right to control popular education.

Not only the religious, but the liberal Conservative press of the Province join in the outcry, that their rights have been invaded by recent legislation. In what respect, then? Surely, it must have been by Imperial legislation, for the end and object, the Parliament of the Province of Quebec seems to have in view, is the consolidation of clerical powers over all the social institutions in the Province, and the establishment of what they are pleased to term their national faith over the ruin of every other.

In corroboration of the remarks already made, that all the Bishops in the Province, the Clergy and laity fully concurred in the obnoxious principles laid down in the Programme, but merely differed as to how the reforms based on them should originate, it is sufficient to refer to the columns of the *Minerve*, the organ of the Liberal Conservative party, of the Government of Quebec, and the French Canadian representation in the Dominion Parliament.

" The *Minerve* promises, in the name of the Conservative party, to grant to the bishops the alterations they may desire in some of our civil laws." * * * * On the 30th May, 1870, it said : " All concessions which the religious authorities will demand from the laity they will not fail to receive with good graces, because they will demand them with good graces. It is against unauthorized demands of concessions made by an unauthorized authority, against which we protest." On the 15th June last, it said : " We are sufficiently acquainted with our legislators to know that the part of the law which relates to Catholics will be promptly corrected when the *Court of Rome* will have made known its will." On the 28th April last, it said: "The *Programme* in itself has nothing unusual or extraordinary; it has always entered into the ideas and spirit of the Conservative party to submit to the wishes of our bishops, and what is better, whenever they have asked for reforms the Conservative party has heartily accorded them." On the 12th May the following remarks occur : "The *Programme* has nothing unusual in itself, inasmuch as it tends to confirm our respect for the will of the Episcopacy. It is only its *timeliness*, as well as the character and intention of those who projected it."

It will thus be seen that the *Programme*, against which the English-speaking people of the Province of Quebec justly took offence, met with the approval, not alone of the Bishops, but of the whole Conservative party in that Province. Three of the Bishops and several organs of the Conservate party merely objected to its timeliness; that is to say, the times were not propitious for the arrogance and impertinence of the authorities of the Church of Rome. That they contemplated the utter prostration of Protestant power and authority in the Province ; that they connived at the flagrant spoliation of whatever rights were left to them ; and that they foresaw the establishment of a great Catholic nation in this country they were willing to admit and approve ; but they alone questioned the expediency of making known at present what they seriously and advisedly thought of and projected for the future.

What influence is otherwise to be drawn from the desire so fully expressed by a certain party in the Church to promulgate the doctrines contained in this *Programme*, and of another party to conceal them *for the present* ? Whence the necessity of concealment, if the design were not seriously entertained ? Treason generally hides itself in a multitude of guises ; the worst to be dreaded, for it is the most dangerous, is that which is hedged in by the power of the Papacy, and the watchfulness and precautions of its secret agents !

The reader will very naturally inquire, whether this state of hostility between the Catholics and Protestants arises from religious causes alone. If it were so, possibly the asperities and animosities between rival sects might be assuaged in the course of time, and the evils arising therefrom be alleviated by the returning good sense and moderation of the people. But unfortunately the evil has a deeper root ; it may be traced to differences in nationality as well as religion. It has been already stated, that notwithstanding the kind offices of the English population of Lower Canada toward the French Canadians, and the benevolent intentions of the British Government, respecting them, they had, ever since the Conquest, been a discontented people. They looked upon their fellow colonists of the other extraction, not only as rivals, but as conquerors, and the thirst for revenge dried up and extinguished every good feeling of which they might have been possessed. The spirit of discontent broke out in the war of the American Revolution; it was partially manifested in the war of 1812, and finally culminated in the rebellion of 1837 and 1838. It is unnecessary to dwell upon that long course of factious and turbulent opposition, which the House of Assembly of the Province of Lower Canada supported, on all occasions, by the unswerving suffra-

ges of its constituents of French origin, had manifested toward
the Government and institutions of Great Britain, although it
was from that Government and those institutions, that the Assembly derived its existence and authority, as a constituent part
of the Legislature of Lower Canada. It will be sufficient to
observe that, no opportunity was ever lost sight of by that
body, for arrogating to itself powers and privileges, which were
never intended to be conferred upon it by the Constitution of
the Province; that every exertion was made to subvert that constitution in its fundamental principles ; and that, ultimately,
the legitimate control of the mother country itself was scorn-
fully set at naught. The redress of grievances was the osten-
sible cause assigned, for the unnatural opposition of the French
Canadians. But it was evident to those, who took the pains to
scrutinize their conduct, that without descending into particular details, no redress of grievances, however ample or complete, could ever conciliate into a proper line of duty, a body
of men whose only aims and objects were to conjure up new
grievances the moment an attempt was made on the part of the
Imperial Government to alleviate the old ones; thus laying the
foundation of endless variance between England and its colony. But this was a state of things which could not be long
endured without imminent danger to the integrity of the Empire, and the peace and happiness of one of its most important
provinces. Accordingly, a check was attempted to be placed
on the revolutionary progress of the House of Assembly, and
upon the application of Government, the Imperial Parliament
did not hesitate to vindicate its own authority for the purpose

of preventing a dissolution of civil society in Lower Canada. This determination served to unmask the whole of the projects of the Assembly and its partisans. Thwarted in their legislative capacity, and finding that they could no longer impose upon the credulity of the British Government or Parliament, they had recourse, for the furtherance of their revolutionary designs, to plebeian patronage and popular agitation. They broke out into open rebellion against the Queen's authority in Canada, and that feeling of hostility against the British Crown, which they had nurtured in their bosoms since the Conquest, which they had manifested during the stormy administrations of Sir James Henry Craig and Lord Dalhousie, and which they have shown ever since, became clear and apparent to the most careless observer. It was not a rebellion against the British Government, for infringing on any abstract principal of human rights, it was not a war, which was waged for the redress of what might be considered any real oppression or grievance ; it was a war of races, begun and carried on for supremacy over their rivals. In its incipient stages, it was marked by a degree of ferocity and blood-thirstiness, which never even characterized the wars of England between the rival factions of York and Lancaster. No sooner had the "sons of Liberty," as the French Canadian rebels called themselves, assembled in the early part of October, 1837, than they hoisted the tri-colored flag and issued an "address to the young men of the North American Colonies," containing sentiments well calculated to arouse the fears of every peaceful subject in the Province; and it was the constant endeavour of the whole of these illegal associations to promulgate doctrines of the most dangerous tendency to the peace of society. Young and old were taught to entertain sentiments at variance with the moral and political obligations of British subjects, and adverse to the supremacy of the mother country.·

Partial and corrupt writers among French Canadians and others, may affirm that the rebellion of 1837 and 1838 was undertaken for the redress of grievances, and point to the efforts of Lord Durham and others as the authors of responsible government, what they thought was to be the panacea for all the evils under which the French Canadians fancied that they labored. In answer, it may be said, that the true history of the Canadian Rebellion has never been written ; that it originated in a deep-seated hatred against the English race in Canada ; that it was fostered and encouraged by an insane desire to see the Crown and authority of France supersede that of England in this country ; and that they, even at that early period, contemplated eventually the formation of a Roman Catholic nation on the shores of the St. Lawrence. The murder of Lieutenant Weir, of the 32nd Regiment, has been already mentioned, and the contemplated assassination of several leading citizens of Montreal, a list of whom was found on the person of John McDonell, Advocate, of that city, who was taken prisoner in the early part of the rebellion, detract greatly from that plausible idea so generally inculcated by the advocates of the French Canadian rebel, that the rebellion was undertaken for the redress of grievances which they suffered under British rule. No, it was a war of races, projected and attempted to be carried out for the extermination of British subjects from one of the colonies of England ; and even assassination was not a means to be deprecated provided their ends could be carried out. They failed, for Providence. was in favor of liberty and the right.

And what is to become of this embryo French Canadian and Catholic nation on the shores of the St. Lawrence? That it will ever arrive at maturity or reach anything like colossal pro-proportions is too absurd to be believed. The logic of events points to the predominance of several great powers on the North American continent ; their form of government and social and political institutions may, and probably will, differ, but they will owe their origin to the Anglo-Saxons. Long after the name of New France shall be forgotten in the Province of Quebec, the story of its conquest by the British arms will be recited to listening ears, and the language of Chaucer and of Dryden will never fail to make them remember the glorious achievements of their ancestors.

It will be interesting to enquire what are the views of the French Canadians respecting annexation? Whenever trade becomes depressed, and they lack energy to embark in industrial pursuits, they imagine a change of Government would improve their material condition, and see in the magnified advantages of annexation a *panacea* for all the evils they endure. This remark applies to the discontented only, for idleness and its consequent evils engender a spirit of discontentment ; but the feelings of the French Canadian generally are enlisted against annexation, as will be seen by the following paragraphs from a late work :—

" It is this fidelity of our fathers to their new mother country which preserved us in 1775 and 1812 from being swallowed up in the great American Republic, and, consequently, from all the misfortunes and ruin which accumulated on this people during the four years of civil war, which has just terminated, and the possible consequences of which at present alarm their most enlightened statesmen. What would have become of us if the religion and patriotism of our fathers had not preserved us, a small Canadian people, from annexation with the United States ? If we wish to know it, we have but to visit the old French establishments of Louisiana, Missouri, and Illinois, and we shall there see but a very small number of them speaking French, the language of our fathers ; for in all these old French colonies, the French language is nothing but a foreign language. Alas ! we shall see a very large number who have lost the Catholic faith and have shamefully apostatized, and that it was necessary for all of them to adopt Republican manners and customs, so little in harmony with the proverbial urbanity and politenes of Old France, from which we have descended. In one word, we convince ourselves that it became necessary to pass through the folly and humiliation of a complete national transformation, which is far from being brilliant." * * *
In another part, he says, " Follow them on Sundays you will see that a certain number of them do not frequent any church ; that many, accompanied by their children are attendants at the Methodist and Presbyterian congregations. In visiting at their
4

houses, yon will not fail to become convinced, that they have yielded to American ideas, morals, and usages. Wherefore, I ask you, to what nationality does a French Canadian family belong, who do not speak the French language, who are no longer Catholics, and who have adopted the morals and customs of Americans? What remains to them of the nationality of their ancestors? Nothing. They are Americans and no longer Canadians These explanations of the sense in which we consider the word 'nationality,' will enable us to discover who are our real friends in this point of view and who are the men, who have really at heart our national interests?"

Herein we have the distinct avowals which parenthetically need correction. The author, a distinguished writer, says, " that in 1775 and 1812, they were preserved by the fidelity of " their forefathers from being engulphed by the great Ameri-" can Republic."

History ; the grim pages of truthful history, totally belie this assertion. It was the valour and the undaunted bravery of British soldiers, who, both in 1775 and 1812, saved this country to the British Crown. In the war of the Revolution, it was the heroic Carleton, who, escaping from Montreal, which Montgomery (ingloriously for the boasting and vaunting French Canadians,) triumphantly entered, descended the St. Lawrence in a canoe to Quebec, and there, with the aid of a handful of British troops, kept Montgomery at bay, until the rigour of the climate and the vicissitudes of a long winter's campaign forced his military successors to evacuate the country.

And what of Chateauguay in 1812? Phillip Aubert de

Gaspe, a favorite historian of the French Canadians, whose memoirs have lately been published, says distinctly that grave doubts existed at the time, whether the French Canadians, who never claimed anything but a stratagem in the battle of that name, did not claim more than they deserved, as the Fencibles, a military corps in the pay of the British Government, really out-numbered the few French Canadians, who were present on the occasion. In other words, he, a distinguished author, and very veracious writer, throws doubts on the valour of his fellow-countrymen, whose descendants never cease to talk of the heroic (?) actions of their ancestors on that memorable battle-field.

The truthfulness of these remarks will be apparent from well-established historical reminiscences. In 1775, but one year previously, the so-called "Quebec Act" had been passed by the Imperial Parliament, guaranteeing to the French Canadians, the exercise of their religion, and the use of their language and their laws. They had hitherto been a discontented and unhappy people ; they thought that they writhed under the iron heel of a rapacious conqueror, and notwithstanding the passing of the Quebec Act, (of the provisions of which they were then scarcely cognizant,) they remained with a very few exceptions, passive and indifferent, and as a people, took no part whatever in repelling the invaders from their soil.

In the war of 1812 and 1814, they had been too recently (as they thought,) the victims of persecution under the administration of Sir James Henry Craig, even to enter into the defence of any of His Majesty's possessions in America. The imprisonment of their political chiefs and the suppression of their press by that worthy Governor, a very few years before the war, were sufficient causes for their indifference, if not their apathy and neutrality.

The *paratheosis* being thus concluded, the question must very naturally be recoursed to, what is to become of this *embryo* French Canadian and Catholic nation on the shores of the St. Lawrence? To put it in their own words, (for logically it is tried to be shown, that the French Canadians desire to found a Nation (!) in this country,)—"Our mission as a peo-
" ple has an essentially religious character. Our national hap-
" piness, as well as our eternal happiness, depends upon our
" attachment to the faith of our fathers. As long as we are
" faithful in walking in their ways, Heaven will prosper us, as
" it blessed them ; we shall advance with a firm and sure pace
" towards the accomplishment of our destinies, which are with-
" out doubt, the formation of a *Great Catholic Nation* in the
" rich and fertile valley of the St. Lawrence. (The italics are the
" learned and distinguished authors.) This truth being under-
" stood, clearly shows us the road to follow, even in the most
" difficult times, such as those we are now passing through,
" (in 1866,) It will sustain our courage, even when every-
" thing seems desperate. Let us, therefore, frankly and sin-
" cerely be always Catholics, and regard the future with a full
" and entire confidence."

And what is to *make* of the French Canadians, a great and powerful Catholic (!) Nation on the banks of the St. Lawrence ?

They have not a single element of greatness or power among them. They are an indolent, idle and effeminate people ; they lack the great purposes and energies of commerce ; neither by their moral or intellectual training, are they fit for those contests, in which men come out the victors, through their superior intelligence and unswerving integrity. In the arts and sciences, with very few exceptions, and those hardly worth mentioning, their intellect is dwarfed, their force deteriorated, and their energy impaired. In the palmy days of Dalhousie and Kempt, when centralization was one of the principles in the social economy of the people, there were men, such as the Bedards, Vallieres de St. Real, Papineau and others, who distinguished themselves at the Bar and in the Senate. There were a few eminent doctors, but there were neither sculptors nor painters, authors nor historians. Of late years, Garneau and the Jesuits of the Laval University have contributed some works to the historical literature of the country, but these are so redolent of French authority and anti-British sentiment, that they can hardly be received as the faithful exponents of the truths of Colonial history. Their colleges annually turn out young men, who are pretty well versed in classical literature, mathematics and rhetoric, but what do they do ? They either immediately embark in the pursuits of the learned profession, already too overcrowded, or, yielding to their natural love of indolence, beguile their time away, uselessly, either to themselves or their country. In industrial or agricultural pursuits, they borrow from every one and invent nothing. With very, very few exceptions, their farmers remain cultivating the same soil their ancestors did years before them, without thinking for a moment of enriching or manuring it, or without adopting any of the modern appliances for its improvement or cultivation. In politics they profess to be something, and in religion everything. More than one-fifth part of the working days of the year, are totally absorbed in religious observances, national holidays and festive occasions. They beat the Tyrolese in their love of display, and the Spaniards and Mexicans in their outward show of empty religious ceremonies.

The census of 1861 states that they then numbered nearly a million, (943,253,) of whom it may be safely computed, nearly one-third have emigaated from Canada to the States. Of these, forty thousand were volunteers in the late civil war, of whom about fifteen thousand where killed. Taking into consideration this large emigration, which is constantly increasing, and the ratio of increase of population comparatively with deaths, it may be presumed, that if *correct information* be afforded from the decennial census now being made, the French Canadian population will remain pretty much the same as it was in 1861, and possibly not quite so much.

Their material resources, comparatively with those of their English-speaking fellow-colonists have already been alluded to. How then can they dream of founding a nation without moral energy, intellectual culture or material wealth ? Even if the great Anglo-Saxon family to the South and West of them placidly looked on and witnessed the experiment, time would dissipate their delusion, and they would only afford further living evidence of the fallacy of the idea, that a nation can be built up without those attributes of the human character, which im_ part strength and solidity, or without those moral qualities, which elevate and adorn men.

In a work entitled "New France," which was published by M. Prevost Paradol, and which excited a great deal of attention at the time throughout Europe, he attributed the loss of France's Empire in the Indies and America, not so much to the want of enterprise and energy among his countrymen, as to the superior intelligence and commercial activity of the Anglo-Saxon race.

The French Canadian in wishing to impose a heavy yoke on his Anglo-Saxon countryman with a view to establish a antionality in the Province of Quebec, does not appear to be guided by the counsels of history or the experience of the past. What has become of the French Empire in India which was established at the sacrifice of so much money and blood by Dupleix? What has become of the French Empire in America, which owed its formation to the truly magnificent designs of Colbert? Look at all the colonies of France, with the exception, possibly, of Algeria, and what is their present state and condition? There is not a single sign of material progress or development among them ; they remain in the same stagnant state in which they existed at the period of their formation, without a ray of sunshine to brighten them, or even without a gleam of hope for the future. And what, it may be asked, has become of France itself? A prey to intestine feuds which partly owe their origin to religion, and partly to the passions of the people ; a country, ernst the pride of the civilized world, the seat of the arts and sciences ; the *nucleus* around which the *Savans* of the world assembled, to draw inspiration and learning from its academies and social gatherings. Is it at this moment, when she lies prostrate at the feet of her proud conqueror, that her children in America should seek to transplant on their own soil, the seed which has borne such fruit on the land of their ancestors ? How much did the sacred name of religion, perverted to the base purpose of pandering to human passions and prejudice, enter into the views of those, who sought to establish a republic on the ruins of monarchy ?

And in treating of the social state and condition of the Protestant in the Province of Quebec, has it not been conclusively shown, that under the sacred guise of religion, the French Canadian wishes to acquire political power and prestige? What arm do they use among the ignorant and uneducated to prejudice them against the English in Quebec, to deprive them of their rights and immunities? Do they appeal to their reason or judgment, or to their intolerance or fanaticism? Do they say that their institutions are threatened, or that their religion is assailed ? No, they wish to create a war of races in the Province of Quebec ; and by the annihilation of the Briton, and the destruction of his most cherished interests, pave the way for the establishment of *La grande nation Canadienne* on the shores of the St. Lawrence, with the Roman Catholic religion for its basis, and the Court of Rome for its preceptor and teacher.

It is impossible that the present state and condition of the Protestant in the Province of Quebec can continue for any

length of time : the most trifling incident, the most insignifi-
cant circumstance may awaken a spirit of revenge, which it
might be difficult to overcome.   If once a war of races, or what
is worse, a religious war, were inaugurated, a flame would arise
compared with which the fires of Smithfield, or the massacre
of St. Bartholomew, would be trifling.   It might spread and
encompass the new world in scenes of devastation and ruin.
How, then, is the evil to be alleviated or the apprehension of
evil to be calmed ?   Sensible and judicious men would answer
by moderate counsels, unswerving impartiality, and strict justice to all classes, irrespective of creed, in the government of
the Province of Quebec.   But many will be found who will
cavil at the idea of the possibility of such sentiments entering
into the views of the Quebec government.   What then ?   Is
it by annexation, absorption, or a strong centralized government, that all classes can be protected in their rights and the
cause of law and order be preserved ?

Annexation, which is another word for absorption in the
political dictionary, has its attendant advantages and disadvan-
tages.   To sum them up cursorily.   In a moral and political
point of view, Canada would be in a worse position than she
is at the present day ; commercially she would be the gainer ;
but in an ethnological sense she would derive incalculable
benefits.   The last stronghold which France had in America
yielded to the persevering spirit of the Anglo Saxon race, and
under the same law of social ethics, in which the weaker yields
to the stronger, the French Canadian would lose his autonomy
and become incorporated into the greater number of the ruling

race. Annexation, absorption and affiliation are synonymous terms, or at least, if they do not mean so, (in the case of the French Canadians), they inculcate the same idea. Logically speaking, annexation, with all the burdens it would entail upon us, would be a peaceable means of attaining the same object, for which all the wars the world ever saw, were conceived and accomplished. Mr. *Theophile Gautier*, one of the ablest modern writers France has produced, says "that slavery and war—it is shameful to say so for the sake of humanity—are instruments of education ; they violently mix up people who would never otherwise have seen each other ; and the conquered learns the science of the conquerors. *Inferior species improve themselves by these forced cross-breeds* ; in playing with his barbarous concubine, the white man creates a superior being, who will avenge his mother in the future."

But to the loyal Briton annexation has another meaning, which jars very inharmoniously on his ears. Is it for the sake of improving the condition of eight or nine hundred thousand French Canadians, that the memories and traditions of the past, which are treasured in the hearts of millions of people, are to be forever obliterated and buried? Is it to quiet their animosities, to propitiate their self-love, and to enable them to indulge in their imaginary idea of founding a nation, that we should resort to a remedy which might possibly be worse than the evil, and which might impair that natural feeling of love for his fatherland, which is paramount in the heart of every Briton?

Besides, it may be asked at what period would it be likely

that annexation would cure the evil? Undoubtedly it would do so in time, but when would that time arrive? State governments would be established and state rights maintained. Every public officer would be elected, and the French Canadians being in a majority, they would predominate at all elections. But this would not last forever. Take Louisiana for instance. It was settled by Louis XIV. in 1718. It was ceded to Spain when the East of the Mississippi was given to England in 1763, and restored to France in 1801. The Americans purchased it in 1803, and it became a State in 1812. It will thus be seen that for nearly a century it was the home of the Latin race ; and that for nearly seventy years, belong-, ing to the Americans, it is only at the lapse of that period, it has ceased to be French, and has become American. It requires time to destroy the roots of a well settled nationality ; nations, like individuals, have their peculiar idiosyncracies ; and one of them, the strongest it may be, is to cling with tenacity to the manners and customs, and the laws and usages of their ancestors.

The transition in case of annexation might be more progressive in Canada. There are many worthy Anglo-Saxons in this country who, entertaining a deep-rooted feeling of affection for the land of their forefathers, would willingly encourage annexation, from the belief that its benefits in this direction would be immediate; that the French Canadians would yield at once before the progressive spirit of the American people, and shake off the apathy and stolidity for which they are remarkable. This may be true to a certain extent. The case of Louisiana is not strictly analogous to that of Quebec. Physiologically, the natives of the Northern States of America are a hardier race than those of the South. Their climate has enured them to all the hardships and vicissitudes of commercial and industrial life. It has made them a strong, hardy, and energetic people, while, on the other hand, the native of the South suffers all the lassitude and weakness incident to their tropical region. The woods and forests, and lakes and streams of Canada would allure them from their homes in the Northern States to share in the wealth which would be derived from their perseverance and hard labor. It would not by any means take as long as it did in Louisiana to fill up the Province of Quebec with the courageous and hardworking denizens of the North, who would immigrate into the country with their axe and their ploughshare, to become rich with the fruits of their labor in the forest and the field.

Here it will very naturally be asked, what impediment exists to the ingress of Americans into Canada at the present day' and their participation in the trade and commerce of the country ?

The experience of the last quarter of a century readily furnishes an answer to this question.

History establishes this fact, that a nation will not, to any great extent, trade with the colony of a foreign nation. The American who comes into the Province of Quebec complains of the peculiarities of the laws, and the want of assimilation between the manners and customs of the people. There are many very worthy men, who have embarked in trade, who arrived in Canada with their families and numerous dependents, and who, after having remained here a while and acquired some wealth, returned to the States, there to spend it. But few have remained in the Province of Quebec, at least, and of those all their predilections, habits, and tastes, are utterly estranged from those among whom they dwell.

To resume, the more correct belief is, that while the Province of Quebec would be greatly ameliorated by the presence of Americans, it would not be in this generation that the Protestants would benefit from the effects of annexation. In the course of time their condition, both political and social, would no doubt be greatly removed, but its effects would not be so immediate as its advocates pretend.

In the meantime, *"hope deferred maketh the heart sick,"* and is it to be expected that over a quarter of a million of British born subjects of Her Majesty will bide the course of time, and calmly and quietly put up with the " stings and arrows of an outrageous fortune," which may be daily and hourly hurled at them at the hands of an ignorant and bigoted people?

History, which as Lord Bolingbroke said, is philosophy teaching by example, proves [the contrary. The spirit, which was evoked during the Rebellion, and which culminated in the burning of the Parliament House in 1849, and the *sudden*, but very *determined* maner in which the Gavazzi riots were quelled by the Protestants of Montreal, and which for ever should immortalize the heroes of Beaver Hall, has not been quenched yet. It may slumber, and for the sake of humanity, it is to be hoped that there will never again be an occasion for its manifestation ; but the truth must be told, the spirit exists, and cannot be rebuked by the force of numbers, or the aid of any military body in support of those numbers.

It thus behoves the true lover of peace to devise some means or mode of action whereby this anomalous state of things, in so far as the Protestant is concerned, should at once and for ever cease to exist. If the evils be of long continuance, the wounds will sink more deeply into the heart of every Briton in Canada, and it will take a long time to eradicate the memory of them.

It has been shown from the bare recital of facts in these pages, that the Roman Catholic *Programme* of the Episcopacy of the Province of Quebec was intended as an insult to the intelligence and love of constitutional liberty of Her Majesty's Protestant subjects in that province. That such was the intention is manifest from the whole context of circumstances under which it was written and promulgated. When learned men, like the Bishops of the Province of Quebec agree in its sentiments, but differ only as to the expediency and *timeliness* of its publication, it is apparent that they themselves considered it to be an insult to their fellow-countrymen of a different creed from their own, who were living in the Province. It may by some be considered as a very harmless production, and reflecting and sensible men may possibly agree in that construction of it ; but the danger consists in the effect it might have on the masses, who do not arrive at conclusions by any slow process of reasoning. Once their passions are excited, it is difficult to allay them ; and what security is there that other and more dangerous publications emanating from the same source may not influence them to such an extent, that they might become perfectly uncontrollable. Besides, the Protestants are a sensitive and high-minded people ; slow to offer offence, they are quick at resenting it, and when they make the effort, it generally proves to be sure and effectual. To avoid this evil, the Roman Catholic ecclesiastical authorities, from whom better things should be expected, should themselves set the example of mutual forbearance and good-will. They should avoid creating strife among the different classes of the people, but when we find them, as we have done on this occasion, spreading a firebrand among them, it is high time they should be rebuked and made to appreciate the fact that the Protestants in the Province of Quebec, though numerically their inferior, are in point of wealth, intelligence and social position eminently their superiors.

The idea of consolidating the British North American Provinces into a great power on this continent was remarkable for the grandeur of its conception ; as a counterpoise to the , spread of democratic principles, it cannot fail to attain its end, and in order that it should become an accomplished fact, it needs a fair trial, without any clog to impede the working of the system. Besides the manifest advantages it will confer on British subjects in Canada, it will be the means of holding in check the tendency of republicans to launch forth into that licentiousness, which is the usual concomitant of democratic institutions. As a refuge for political offenders, it has already, in the case of the Southern refugees, been proved efficacious ;

and the occasion may again and again arise, when an asylum might be required in either country to protect men from real or fancied grievances they may suffer in their own.

But there are several provisions in the British North America Act of 1867, which militate against the rights and liberties of the English speaking subjects of Her Majesty in the Province of Quebec. There does not appear to have been that calmness and deliberation displayed in the preparation of the Act, which its importance deserved, and its future consequences on the different classes of the population called for. It was intended to estabish a form of government which was to subsist for ages, for whether it would merge into a viceroyalty under the protection of England or into a limited monarchy, its character for permanence and durability was essentially contemplated.

Before continuing the subject, it may be advisable to pass in review the proceedings by which the Union Act came into operation.

At the Charlottetown Conference, which was held in September, 1864, the subject of a *legislative* union of the Provinces being mooted, the Lower Canadian delegates declared that not being authorized to consider the question of a *legislative* union, they could only be informally present. The conference was then adjourned to the 10th October to meet in Quebec. It sat some eighteen days, and the result of their deliberations were the famous " Seventy-two resolutions " the Address to the Crown on which was sanctioned by the following vote in the Legislative Assembly, on the 10th March, 1865. The resolutions were carried by a vote of 91 to 33. Of the 91 who supported the resolutions, there were 54 from Upper Canada, and 37 from Lower Canada; while 25 from Lower Canada, and 8 only from Upper Canada, made up the 33 who opposed them. They again met in England, when Lower Canada was represented by the Hon. G. E. Cartier, A. T. Galt, and H. L. Langevin. Of these, the former and the latter are Roman Catholics, while Mr. Galt being a Protestant, it may fairly be questioned whether he was a fitting representative of the Protestant section of the community in Lower Canada. That both the delegates in Quebec and those in London exercised a most powerful influence in favour of Roman Catholic interests, without much counteracting weight on the side of the Protestants, seems to be apparent from the carelessness with which the interests of the latter were regarded by the delegates. It has already been shown, how eager the Roman Catholic clergy were in Lower Canada to establish the federal union, and that after having consulted the Roman authorities, how readily they gave their adhesion to the doctrine of ceding the right of making laws on the subject of divorce to the Federal Parliament. They yielded this point solely for the purpose, (as has been before remarked), of establishing a power in the Province of Quebec, by means of which they could obtain the ascendancy over the Protestant element in that Province. Of course, the two Catholic delegates at the Westminster Hotel impressed on the minds of the statesmen of England, that the measure was popular amongst all classes in Lower Canada, a statement in which

5

Mr. Galt, with his characteristic politeness and urbanity may have concurred; yet it may be faithfully asserted, that there were a few far seeing statesmen in England, who not only doubted the policy of the measure but actually foresaw its disastrous results to Anglo-Saxon and Protestant interests in the Province of Quebec. That their views were correct, and that their worst apprehensions may be possibly realized, is apparent from the actual state of affairs in the Province.

It is true, as a well known author has asserted, that " party government had at that period (1864) become well nigh impossible in United Canada, and ministry after ministry had to retire from the seemingly hopeless attempt at carrying on the government, when on the defeat of the Taché-Macdonald ministry, in June 1864, overtures were made by the leaders of the Reform party to the Hon. John A. Macdonald, with a view to the settlement of the sectional difficulties by the adoption of a federative system, applying either to Canada or to all the British North American Provinces. These overtures were cordially received, and the result was the formation of a coalition government, pledged to the introduction of the federal system."

It will thus be seen that the Delegates at Charlottetown could not contemplate for a moment the establishment of a Legislative Union—Lower Canada had too recently emerged from a controversy, which had been carried on for years with the advocates of Representation by Population, to entertain for a moment the idea of a still larger union than that which had existed between Upper and Lower Canada. The French

Canadians feared the ascendancy of the Anglo-Saxon element in an assembly constituted for Legislative purposes, which might interfere with their cherished ideas respecting their language, religion, and laws. Consequently, a Federal Government was established, and their very first act carried through by their representatives in the Ministry at Ottawa, was to name a French Canadian Lieutenant Governor for the Province of Quebec, who was remarkable only for his steadfastness to the cause of the Roman Catholic Clergy ; for his extreme views in favor of the nationality of his fellow-countrymen ; and, it may be added, for his intolerance and bigotry. Neither intellectually, morally, nor socially, was he qualified to fill the first position in a British Colony, under the domination of the British Crown.

Besides the manifest injustice to Protestant interests in excluding other constituencies from the second schedule mentioned in the 8oth section of the Act, to which allusion has already been made, its framers took especial care to comprise within the exclusive powers of the Provincial Legislatures, the right to legislate respecting the "solemnization of marriage in the Province," and "property and civil rights in the Province." Under these powers, as has before been observed, the foulest wrongs may be perpetrated, for when the right is conferred, it is only a question of expediency with them, when it should be exercised. There is nothing which is held so sacred in the eyes of all civilized communities as the right and liberty to govern their own marriage ceremonies, and to establish the personal status of their members. This has been rendered liable to be abused through the intolerant spirit of an adverse religious majority, whose decision would be final, there being no appeal from the action of the Legislature. It is on this account that the Roman Catholic Clergy are now making urgent demands on their *mandataries* both in the Ministry and Parliament, to alter the laws relating to the solemnization of the marriage ceremony, and to make other changes in the civil registers of the Province. What may be the effect of these alterations in the existing law of the Province on the interest of the Protestant section of the community, remains to be determined.

The Delegates both to the Charlottetown Conference and that which was held at Quebec, insisted on the use of the French language in the debates of the houses of the Parliament of Canada and of the houses of the Legislature of Quebec, and under the operation of the 133d section of the Union Act, both those languages *shall* be used in the respective records and journals of those houses ; and either of those languages may be used by any person or in any pleading or process in or issuing from any Court in Canada, and in or from all or any of the Courts of Quebec."

Under the operation of this section, French interests have been so far protected by the Delegates, that, at an enormous expense to the Dominion, and to gratify the vanity and self-love of the French Canadians, the French language has been placed on the same footing in a British Colony, as the language of our forefathers. On no consideration of principle or social economy ought this to have been tolerated, in so far as the

Legislature of the Dominion of Canada was concerned. Not alone by ministering to the arrogance and ignorance of the population of Quebec, but by imbuing their minds with an idea of equality of rights between the English and French, is this measure to be deprecated and to be considered both impolitic and unwise. It is unjust also, for should other nationalities obtain a social position in Canada, equal in point of number and strength to the French Canadians, they also would be entitled to the use of their languages in the Parliament, and to have their records and journals written in the idioms most familiar to them. The views of the Delegates would have been quite sufficiently cosmopolitan in restricting all nationalities to the use of the English language, which should be spoken by every man who claims to be intelligent, no matter in what quarter of the world he may abide. The only remedy for the evils which may befal the Protestants of Quebec would be the repeal of the British North America Act, in so far as their rights and interests may be affected, and *the abolition of the use of the French language in the Parliaments of the Dominion.* If this colony remain a dependency of the British Crown, its form of Government should be assimilated to that of England as much as possible. The power of appointment to all offices in the Dominion should be vested in the Governor-General, instead of the Local Governor, who (as in the case of Quebec) may use it for the purpose of rewarding political supporters *belonging to his nation*, and not according to the true intent and spirit of the Imperial Act which conferred it upon him. Surely if the Queen of England has the right of nominating to office

in the British Isles, and in many other portions of her Dominion, there are additional reasons why that right should in this
country be conferred solely on the Governor-General. Centralization of power and authority is more required in a sparsely
populated country such as Canada, than it is in England,
where it is more difficult to perform acts of administration
among the millions, who constitute its population.

We have thus far pointed out the present attitude of the
French Canadian and Roman Catholic towards his fellow
countryman of British and Protestant extraction. We have
shown that in their design to establish *la grande Nation Canadienne*, on the banks of the St. Lawrence, they heed not the
rights or liberties of any other class of the people; that from
their self-sufficiency and arrogance they would spurn every
English speaking colonist, who would dare to interfere with
their purposes to re-establish an effete and extinguished nationality in Canada. We have signalized their weak and covert
attempts to try and triumph for a moment over a brave and
generous people, who have sustained a multitude of wrongs at
their hands, without a word of complaint or remonstrance.
We have shown how the English colonist in the Province of
Quebec, while peaceably pursuing his duties, both as a citizen
and a man, has had his prospects injured and thwarted, and
his happiness even destroyed through religious intolerance and
bigotry! *And we have barely hinted at the remedy.* In conclusion, we shall now take a glance (imperfect though it may
be) at the improbability of the French race ever again holding
a political position *in any part* of the Continent of America.

The day of their supremacy has passed, never again to return !

And what are the causes of this loss of power and *prestige?* Look at a map of the western world and compare it with one that may have been published before the battle of Louisburg. What do you find ? The whole of the North American Continent, with the exception of a very few British and Dutch colonies, in the hands of the French, yielding allegiance to the French Crown, and with the *fleur de luys*, emblazoning their national flag. What do you *now* find ? Nearly the whole of that large space of the earth's possessions, containing a homogeneous people, boasting of their Anglo-Saxon ancestry, speaking their language, obeying their laws, and loving the old manners, traditions, and customs of their forefathers ! St. George and the Dragon of England, with the stars of the Republic, have replaced the boasted *fleur de luys* of France !

Again, what is the cause ? One of the most accomplished French writers (Prevost Paradol of the French Academy) gives it in a few words,—" Even at the present day, a book written in the English language, is read by an infinitely larger number of human beings, than if it had been written in our own language, and it is in English that the mariner is saluted at every point of the habitable globe." In other words, literature and commerce have been the great civilizing agents, which Providence has placed in the hands of the Anglo-Saxon race to conquer and subdue the world. With the Bible in the one hand, and the compass in the other, the Anglo-Saxon has performed and is performing the Divine mission of enlightening and civilizing the whole human race !

Another cause of French humiliation in the world of commerce are their constant wars and revolutions. To this may be added, their addiction to the higher branches of science; their academies are resplendent with men of genius and learning ; their schools abound with *savans*, from whom the English have borrowed, and delight to borrow, but their love of isolation, and their ignorance of the outer world, of its languages and its customs, have interposed an impenetrable barrier against any great progress in either navigation or commerce. How rapidly has been the transition ! From being the foremost nation of Europe in national and commercial enterprises, they have descended to such an inferior scale in the commerce of the world, that their flag is now comparatively unnoticed in any part of it. Their former military and naval superiority over their rival Latin races has been overshadowed by equally great triumphs in the realms of science and of art.

For nearly two centuries France maintained its authority in San Domingo, one of the finest islands in the Caribean Sea, and now we find the Anglo-Saxon race wishing to purchase, if they cannot conquer it. In Mexico it emitted its last expiring throe for the re-establishment of its empire in America, and what has been the result? The misfortunes of Maximilian and Carlotta, over whom history will never cease to throw a shade of romance, are there, as an appalling proof of the destiny (which Divine Providence seems to have ordained) of the French race on the continent. The small island of Martinique and French Guiana are all that is left of that proud empire, which the great Colbert, the minister of Louis XVI, predicted would overshadow the new world.

It is apparent to every historian that the progress of the Anglo-Saxon race on this continent especially, has kept pace with the decadence of the Latin race—with the exception of the·Spaniards in South America and Cuba, whose energies both mental and physical, seem to be waning, and who can hardly be regarded with the same pride as their ancestors of old. No European race seems to prosper on this continent, but those who are descended from the Saxon and the Celt.

And what a proud position the Dominion of Canada will sustain in its rivalry with the United States of America for the commerce of a great part of the world? With their compe: ting railways, they will stretch out their arms and grasp the wealth of a prosperous trade with India and China, and the Australian colonies and the islands of the Southern Ocean. There will be no bounds to their material progress and prosperity, but those which they themselves will create. There will be no limit to their ambition, as far as space is concerned. The wealth of the Indies and the "road to China," for which statesmen and navigators of every country in the world sighed in vain, will lie at their feet; and besides wealth, their children and their children's children will look wtih honor and with pride on the efforts of their forefathers to obtain the prize, the fruits of which they will enjoy.

And shall this proud future be marred by the efforts of any class or section of Canadians, who would deprive us of that unity, so essential to the happiness of individuals as of nations?

Shall religious jars and national feuds be suffered to impair that noble spirit of enterprise and commercial activity, which bids fair to invest us with all the elements of a nation's growth and prosperity? Let the French Canadians sink the ideas of nationality and religion in an earnest and well-felt desire to out-rival and surpass their fellow-countrymen of other origins, in the sciences and the arts of peace and commerce ; and here-after in the national greatness and glory, which may be expected to await our newly established Dominion, they will take equal pride with men of every other country and creed in the Province.

www.ingramcontent.com/pod-product-compliance
Lightning Source LLC
Chambersburg PA
CBHW021531270326
41930CB00008B/1190